Dedicated to:
The Palmieri Family

Written by: Abigail Gartland

Hello, my name is St. Pope John Paul II!

I was born in Poland in 1920!

I had a very deep love for Jesus from the time I was a little boy.

My mom died when I was very young, and two of my siblings also died. I was so sad.

My faith helped me to know that they were with Jesus.

While I was growing up, I loved playing outside, writing and the theatre.

In 1939, my home in Poland was invaded, so I entered into the seminary in secret.

I kept it a secret because there were people who didn't want others to love Jesus.

I studied God's word, and became a priest.

I loved teaching and sharing everything I knew about Jesus.

I worked to teach all people in the world that Jesus loves them.

I became Pope John Paul II in 1978 and shared the Word of God with every nation.

I was the pope for almost 27 years!

Do you want to be more like me?

You can celebrate my feast day with me on October 22nd.

I am the patron saint of young people and families.

I pray for you and your family every day.

St. John Paul II, pray for us!

Copyright:

Clipart: © PentoolPixie © LimeandKiwiDesigns
Licensed purchased: 1/10/2024

About the Author
Abigail Gartland

I love the saints and I love my faith. The idea for sharing the stories of the saints with little ones came when my dear friends were expecting their first baby. I wanted to create something as unique and special as our friendship. Each book is dedicated to very special people and groups who have enriched my faith in different ways. I am blessed to write these stories and appreciate the unending support of my family and friends. When I am not writing, I am a middle school teacher. I hope you enjoy these stories. I pray for each and every person who opens one of my books to learn more about the saints.

Abbie

www.ingramcontent.com/pod-product-compliance
Lightning Source LLC
LaVergne TN
LVHW061633070526
838199LV00071B/6662